My Kind *of*
GARDEN

My Kind *of* GARDEN

*Photographs & Insights
on Creating a Personal Garden*

RICHARD W. BROWN

A Frances Tenenbaum Book

HOUGHTON MIFFLIN COMPANY

Boston   New York   1997

For information about permission to
reproduce selections from this book, write to
Permissions, Houghton Mifflin Company,
215 Park Avenue South, New York, New York 10003.

For information about this and other Houghton Mifflin
trade and reference books and multimedia products, visit
The Bookstore at Houghton Mifflin on the World Wide Web
at http://www.hmco.com/trade/.

Library of Congress Cataloging-in-Publication Data
is available

Printed in Italy

SFE 10 9 8 7 6 5 4 3 2 1

Book design by Susan McClellan

Illustrations by Richard W. Brown

Color separations, printing, and binding by Sfera

Cover photograph © by Richard W. Brown

For my mother and father,
who gave me my stubborn Yankee roots,
and with patience and care
helped them to grow

Contents

GARDEN MOMENTS

Many people who love flowers and wish to do some practical gardening are at their wits' end to know what to do and how to begin. Like a person who is on skates for the first time, they feel that, what with the bright steel runners, and the slippery surface, and the sense of helplessness, there are more ways of tumbling about than of progressing safely in any one direction.

~ GERTRUDE JEKYLL

*M*Y EDUCATION AS A GARDENER began not with a trowel but with a camera. Perhaps because recognizing special moments is the essence of photography, I became drawn to gardens and their fleeting spectacle as a subject and practiced a hands-off kind of gardening in which I harvested with my camera what others had sown. The flowers and plants, the style and history, the eccentricity, the surprises, were all inspiration for my lens. I spent countless hours as I worked, just looking and soaking in all of the elements that worked together to make certain gardens such compelling creations. Being cursed (or blessed?) with an active imagination as well as a strong visual bent, I soon formed a wish list of what most appealed to me – of what would ideally go into my kind of garden if I had the time and the knowledge and the wherewithal to make such dreams come true.

More realistically, and in self-defense, I began to familiarize myself with the vast array of flora that I was so blissfully and ignorantly pho-

PAGE 8: *The knot garden, Cranborne Manor, Dorset, England.*

OPPOSITE: *Double peony 'Judy Ann'.*

tographing. Inevitably, while I was being shown around a celebrated garden by some master plantsman or esteemed horticulturalist, there would be a pause and the dreaded question "The *Sidalcea malvifloras* are putting on quite a show, don't you think?" and all I could do was nod enthusiastically and pray I was at least looking in the general vicinity of the species in question. Or my guide would ask, "What do you think is the problem with that *Campanula latifolia* over there?" and I would try to bluff my way through with "Boy, I don't know, mine have been doing exactly the same thing."

By degrees, my horticultural knowledge increased and my intimidation subsided. One April day, without fanfare, I took the plunge. I walked up the ramp to my old Vermont cow barn, where over the years an assortment of hoes, rakes, and shovels had accumulated in a corner, and picked out a rusted but sturdy-looking spade. Returning to the yard, I found a likely spot and began digging up a bed for a few perennials. My checkered gardening career had begun.

One of my first discoveries was that gardening is not for the lazy. All those books with titles like *The 20-Minute Gardener* or *Gardening Made Easy* to the contrary, gardening is hard, hard work. The final result is directly proportional to the amount of physical and mental exhaustion achieved. Gardeners are always going on about how it's their relaxation, their exercise, their therapy – it's really not work at all. That's all lies; they're just so obsessed they don't notice the punishment they're taking. The human body was not designed to kneel endlessly, or crawl around on all fours for hours at a time under the baking sun, or bend interminably at the waist pulling up weeds and pottering over plants. I have observed these people at nurseries and garden centers limping about with gimpy knees, blistered, sunburned necks, backs bent at odd angles, and that driven, fixated look in their eyes – all from too much time spent relaxing in their gardens.

While I had always been impressed by what others had accomplished, I now photographed gardens with a better understanding and newfound admiration for the Herculean labors that went into their creation – which is why you won't see a single photograph of my gar-

PREVIOUS SPREAD:
*The lupine meadow,
Les Quatre Vents, Quebec.*

OPPOSITE: *Hollyhocks
growing outside the
Cornish, New Hampshire,
studio of the sculptor
Augustus Saint-Gaudens.*

den in this book. It is – how shall I put it kindly? – still too immature, too incomplete, too (I admit it) embarrassing. If this were the sort of book that has before and after pictures, my garden could provide most of the "befores" but very few "afters." What you will find are photographs of far better examples of the gardener's art and a discussion of the elements and principles of gardening gleaned through looking at what these truly gifted gardeners have done, tempered by my own experiences in creating a small garden in northern Vermont.

BECAUSE A GARDEN IS CONSTANTLY CHANGING, serious and successful gardeners like to talk about their garden's moments. For such talented and hardworking souls, there are indeed quintessential times when particular flowers are at their pinnacle of bloom – the iris moment, say, or the rose moment. Or there are times when everything is as it should be in a garden, and the entire effect delights the senses. The perennial border is harmonious, weed-free, and overflowing, the sunlight is dappled and mellow, there is birdsong, only a trifling breeze, and even the insects are benign: honeybees, swallowtails, dragonflies, ladybugs.

My garden's best moment, in contrast, is usually around January twentieth, the three-feet-of-snow moment, when everything is hidden, smoothed over, and left to the imagination. In fact, there are a lot of downright unpleasant moments in my garden – the mosquito moment, for instance, or the woodchuck moment, or the everything-laid-flat-by-the-rampaging-Holsteins moment. Yet even in my indifferent garden, there are good moments, even perfect ones, when heavy-budded peonies open in unison and dazzle the eye with their full, feathered blooms or the scent of mock orange hangs in the evening air with the soft, sad sweetness of a childhood memory. These are the moments, of course, that make it all worthwhile, that make up for all the frustrations and disappointments and make us spend so much time on our hands and knees, digging in the dirt.

Chapter I

A Good Plan

There wants a good plan, good execution, a perfect knowledge

of the country . . . an infinite delicacy in the planting.

~ LANCELOT "CAPABILITY" BROWN

A LANDSCAPE HAS A DEFINITE PERSONALITY, which every good gardener encourages and nurtures. The more we try to subvert the natural genius of a place, the more struggle and disappointment will follow. It's like trying to force a child who is very musical and romantic by nature, who wants to be the next Cole Porter, to go to accounting school and join the family firm. The outcome is bound to be failure and misery.

Of course, this intrinsic personality is largely influenced by physical and climatic features. Steep stony terrain naturally leads toward some sort of rock or alpine garden, while a vast expanse of fertile, well-drained loam offers many more options. Wet ground is the promised land as far as primula and yellow flag are concerned, while dry ground is just the thing for succulents. Basically we want our plants to feel at home and not pine away for conditions more to their liking. I suppose with enough effort and money and mulch, tender roses could be grown in International Falls, Minnesota. At least Japanese beetles, who enjoy year-round winter sports even less than 'Peace' roses do, wouldn't be a problem, but those poor tortured plants would inevitably have the miserable and dejected look of Siberian exiles.

This is a blatantly obvious rule of gardening, but it is not hard to un-

derstand why we all choose to ignore it from time to time. Some plants are so uniquely seductive and such strong personal favorites that we willingly take leave of our senses.

I've always had an inordinate weakness for boxwood, for example. It's not so much the superb architectural qualities of this shrub, or even the rich glossy green of its foliage; it's the intoxicating smell of the stuff, that unique pungent evergreen essence which brings back memories of warm and languid afternoons idled away in old southern gardens. Naturally I wanted a few boxwoods around my place to give me such Proustian rushes whenever I caught a whiff of them. And naturally I chose to ignore the fact that I hadn't seen a boxwood within 150 miles of northeastern Vermont.

My first attempt involved two classic English boxwoods, which I planted on either side of the granite porch steps so I could be transported by their fragrance as I whiled away the evening in the old Boston rocker, watching the Jersey heifers graze under the apple trees while the fireflies came out. The next spring the shrubs were stone dead, of course, so I yanked them out and planted two more, and did all those things in the fall with stakes and burlap and hay and old leaves that you're supposed to do to keep such southern belles from languishing in our cruel northern clime. When I unmummified them the following May, they were every bit as dead as their predecessors.

Next I tried two Korean boxwoods that were rumored to be impervious to subzero temperatures. With a minimum of fuss they actually wintered over, but flourish they did not. By the end of May, all the old standby northern Vermont plants, plants that had actually enjoyed their arctic hibernation, were wildly bursting forth with impossibly green shoots and leaves and buds, but the Korean boxes, upon which I had placed such fond hopes, sulked defiantly. They displayed a surly nasty deadish khaki color that no amount of boxwood aroma could make up for. By midsummer they had fully recovered, but it was too late. I was thoroughly disenchanted. There is something about

PAGE 16: *North Hill, Vermont.*

OPPOSITE AND ABOVE: *Pungent boxwood, tree peonies, and Darwin tulips flourish in a recreated eighteenth-century garden, Colonial Williamsburg, Virginia.*

a half-dead-looking plant in the midst of riotous spring growth that drags down the whole effect. It's like talking to a beautiful woman with a bit of spinach caught in her teeth. Try as you might to look elsewhere, your eye goes right to it.

Then too, even when the boxwoods had caught up with the rest of the garden, there was something not quite right about them. They looked too refined, too civilized, too – why should I have been surprised? – southern for my plain old Yankee farmhouse. Which brings us to another aspect of sensible garden planning: regional and cultural suitability. I want to be open-minded about this, but having seen so many lost-looking Japanese stone lanterns that have wandered awfully far from home and Italian Renaissance cherubs that have alighted among the marigolds like visitors from another planet, I think a gardener's first instinct should be to create a garden that is true in spirit to the culture and history of the surrounding region – one that at least has some echoes of what has come before and is not a haphazard pastiche of imported styles and clichés.

ABOVE: *A Shinto temple path, Kyoto, Japan.*

OPPOSITE: *In the Hall garden, an eastern aesthetic is skillfully combined with the raw materials of the Maine coast – ferns, moss, and weathered granite.*

Notice I said first instinct. There are many gardens that ignore this bit of common sense brilliantly. Consider the wonderful country house and garden in the south of England called Sizencote, built at the same time as the Brighton Pavilion, when all things Indian were the rage. It's like a bit of the Taj Mahal set down in the middle of the Cotswold countryside, but it is charming and it works – perhaps more so now than when it was first created, for it has aged well. No doubt Sizencote's exotic plantings and garden ornaments with their giant twining serpents and fanciful Mogul arches have mellowed over the years and become a more convincing part of the landscape. And of course the English have this cult of eccentricity to make it all seem more fitting.

CLOSER TO HOME, AND ON A SMALLER SCALE, the Hall garden, in Northeast Harbor, Maine, combines elements of the Japanese garden aesthetic with the haunting natural beauty of the area in a

thoroughly convincing manner. In an undisturbed corner of the forest, at the very edge of the Atlantic, a massive weathered oblong of granite has been set in the ground like an ancient dolmen. Its angle and shape echo the surrounding black spruce and birch, and at its base native ferns and mosses have been informally arranged in emulation of a Japanese temple garden. It is Ryoan-Ji with a Maine accent. When the fog drifts in from the ocean and the cool air is filled with the soothing sound of water dripping off the spruce boughs and the muffled lapping of the waves below, it is as spiritual and contemplative a garden as any in Kyoto. It is successful because a literal recreation of a Japanese garden wasn't forced upon the landscape. Rather, the elements that were already present were recognized and enhanced and the garden reflects the true spirit of the place.

PERHAPS I SOUND TOO DOGMATIC on this subject. but I speak from bitter experience. As a garden photographer, I have spent a huge amount of time in very grand and impressive gardens. As you might imagine, after a few months of photographing Versailles and Knightshayes Court, Keukenhof, Bagatelle, and Villa d'Este, I would return to my modest Vermont garden with visions of parterres and allees, sparkling water features and classical statuary clouding my judgment. Not that I was thinking of attempting anything so grandiose, of course, but I was awed by all the horticultural and ornamental riches I had seen in my travels, and the simple charms of the plantings that graced my back yard, many of which had been there for nearly a century, were lost to my jaded eyes.

 I decided to create a paved area next to the house – what most Americans would call a brick patio but I insisted on calling a terrace, because that sounded more refined – surrounded by a low wall, with some sort of water activity at the far end. There would be a large tree with a table under it where people would gather and shell peas from the vegetable garden or husk just-picked sweet corn or whatever, and take

PREVIOUS SPREAD AND OPPOSITE: *The Bagatelle rose pergola, Paris, and the Neptune Basin, Versailles — the sort of European garden wonders that led me astray.*

ABOVE: *Brick terrace, Winterthur, Delaware.*

OPPOSITE: *The Schoellkopf garden in western Connecticut, sophisticated yet still appropriately rural in feeling.*

refreshments and be convivial and witty, or relaxed and indolent as in a turn-of-the-century painting by William Merritt Chase.

Never mind that there wasn't any water where the water feature was supposed to go, or any large tree to shade the table, or any vegetable garden to supply the peas and corn, or, especially, any spare time in which to be indolent à la William Merritt Chase. At that time there wasn't even a door on that side of the house to get to the "terrace," so it was a pretty long hike around the end of the garage, which wasn't very handy or elegant. (Eventually, the door did get put in.)

Out went all the old standbys – the clumps of orange daylilies, the bed of *Hydrangea grandiflora*, the Siberian iris, and even the ancient tangled thicket of twenty-foot-high mock orange – all to be replaced by a sea of brick lapping at my sturdy granite foundation. After several months of anxiety, toil, and sweat, my garden room, as such things are wont to be called, was finished. It wasn't completely furnished yet. The shade tree still had to be found and moved into its allotted spot and the water feature still splashed and sparkled only in my imagination, but I decided to have a few friends over to celebrate anyhow.

"It's very lovely, Richard," remarked a neighbor, an honest-to-God poet whom I had invited to make sure the conversation would be convivial and witty enough, "but isn't it awfully, ah . . ." – poets always search for the perfect word – "*urban?*"

She was absolutely right, of course, and over the past twelve years I have struggled and struggled to try to blend this misplaced urban slab of brick into its thoroughly rural setting. It would look fine in Savannah or San Francisco, but it's all wrong in the wilds of Vermont. I've tried to soften the edges with roses and perennials, torn up bricks here and there, and tucked in bits of moss and creeping thyme and ground phlox, candytuft and artemisia to give it that mellow Fall-of-Empire look. But I doubt that any amount of thyme or time will ever heal this wound.

ACTUALLY, I DID GET A FEW THINGS RIGHT. The surrounding walls are made of weathered fieldstone hauled from my pastures and look en-

tirely fitting. Even the water feature (of which you'll hear a good deal later), when it was finally constructed, proved to be a real gem – except that the cows, who are too lazy to walk down to the brook for their water, keep trying to get at it and have caused several unpleasant incidents. But how much simpler it would have been, how much less frustrating, to have planned something more appropriate, more in keeping with the thoroughly rural nature of the site in the first place.

So, fair warning. Entertain in your mind's eye all the Japanese pagodas, riotous twenty-foot-wide English perennial beds, and Italian marble swains and shepherdesses you wish, but before you take shovel or wheelbarrow or checkbook in hand, be sure you've gotten to know your garden spot's true personality.

*At Newton Vineyards in
California's Napa Valley,
a formal garden has been
created over the chardonnay
cellar. Mediterranean in
feeling, it is well suited
to the climate and the
mountainous vineyards
that surround it.*

CHAPTER II

GARDEN BONES

One wide paved walk, one lily pool as large as can be

managed, one border as wide as feasible, and an enclosure of

shrubs notable for foliage and texture and flower or fruit . . .

and the bones are cast, as you might say.

~ HENRY MITCHELL

THE FIRST TIME I OVERHEARD a couple talking in hushed tones about a garden's bones, an image of some past mayhem or foul play sprang to mind (just the sort of spooky, macabre thing you want to imagine in an old estate garden), and I was sadly disappointed to learn that they were discussing its structure instead. I have since learned, in fact, that gardeners talk a great deal about bones, and justifiably so, for bones are as essential to a successful garden as sunlight and rain.

Bones are the structural skeleton, so to speak, of the garden – the various walls and walkways, the steps and changing levels, the pergolas, arbors, and trelliswork that give the garden form and architectural substance. They provide the formality and hard edges that are a perfect foil for the softer, more "natural" plants. When masterfully done, this mixing of differences produces an eminently pleasing synergy. Such sympathetic joinings of opposites are, after all, the essence of life – yin and yang, male and female, hot, tart apple pie and cold, sweet vanilla ice cream. The combinations are infinitely better than the individual parts.

At the risk of belaboring this metaphor, I would have to say that the garden path is the all-important backbone and the other architectural fea-

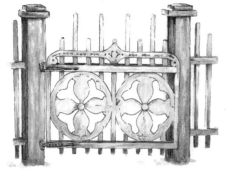

tures are ancillary, ribs or collarbones or whatever. Everything else in the garden depends on the course the path takes; it dictates what goes where and from what angle it will be viewed. Above all, it should promote leisure, a rare and precious commodity. A garden is best experienced at the pace of a very slow walk, with numerous long pauses to enjoy whatever horticultural or decorative treats might lie in store — about the pace of a grazing sheep or a nine-year-old whom you have asked three times to get ready for the school bus. Adequate width is essential. Narrowness causes a hurried, claustrophobic frame of mind.

Whether the path meanders or is ramrod straight, there has to be something at the end of it to arouse our interest, even if it is only a small birdbath or a planting of annuals. That something should tug at our curiosity and invite us to explore. This feeling of invitation is surprisingly easy to achieve. All that is necessary is a bit of structure at several key points along the path to suggest an opening or a doorway left partly open, something that partially hides the eventual goal from view. These structures can be very simple — just two upright evergreens such as cedars or junipers framing an opening, or a simple rustic archway supporting a climbing rose or two.

My first choice, of course, would be a weatherworn old gate, indispensable to a garden that has any pretense to tradition, mystery, or romance. The more ancient and rusted or lichen-encrusted, the better. It should sag a bit, and the hinges should creak reliably. Actually, it shouldn't even swing all the way shut properly. Better if it doesn't, unless rabbits and dogs with unsavory reputations roam the neighborhood. Better to leave it mostly ajar, as if some aged, forgetful gardener who has been in the family's employ for eons left it that way. This effect is irresistible, as an open cupboard door is to a cat.

ANOTHER TRICK THAT HAS BEEN USED BY GARDENERS since time immemorial is to put a little bend about two thirds down the length of the path so that you can't see where it actually ends. This also creates that beckoning quality, that open invitation to come and explore, that is the essential ingredient in any garden path worthy of the name.

ABOVE: *Weed-free paving stones and a brick wall in an enclosed perennial garden, Sissinghurst, England. Its creator, Vita Sackville-West, believed in "the strictest formality of design, with the maximum informality in planting."*

OPPOSITE: *Wrought-iron gate and stucco wall, Charleston, South Carolina.*

Paths paved with old frost-proof brick or flat weathered stones laid in sand are especially handsome – but not maintenance-free. Having often worn the skin off my knuckles weeding witch grass and purslane out of such paving, or risked ostracism by covertly employing chemical warfare to the same end, I have discovered that using a weed-whacker to trim these tenacious miscreants down to nothing several times a season works wonders.

NEXT IN THE WAY OF DESIRABLE GARDEN BONES come the walls. Ideally, somewhere in the garden there should be a walled enclosure to provide that special feeling of apartness and secrecy that can be achieved in no other way. As Gertrude Jekyll somewhat stuffily put it, "Walls are the provider of shelter and privacy which are proper to a garden." It was Frances Hodgson Burnett, however, who captured the true spell of a walled garden in *The Secret Garden:*

It was the sweetest, most mysterious-looking place anyone could imagine ... The high walls which shut it in were covered with the leafless stems of climbing roses, which were so thick that they were matted together ... The sun was shining inside the four walls and the high arch of blue sky over this particular piece of Misselthwaite seemed even more brilliant and soft than it was over the moor ... Everything was strange and silent, and she seemed to be hundreds of miles away from anyone, but somehow she did not feel lonely at all.

ABOVE: *A brick wall shelters climbing roses and delphiniums. Powis Castle, Wales.*

OPPOSITE: *Agecroft Hall, Richmond, Virginia.*

Walls do provide shelter and increased warmth for plants, a stately frame for your horticultural work of art and all that, but it is this delicious feeling of secrecy and mystery, palpable yet unthreatening, that is their greatest worth.

As to the walls themselves, the higher the better, up to a point. You don't want to feel imprisoned. Being built of some sort of masonry seems to be the key; wooden walls are better than none at all, but they don't have quite the same feeling of permanence and solidity. Stone is good, antique brick is the genuine article, and even cinder block, when well disguised with several flaking layers of stucco, can have the right feel (I've seen excellent examples in Charleston and St. Augustine). A little dilapidation doesn't hurt, either. A few missing bricks and chunks of mortar, a slight bend or a crack or two, only add to the charm and give climbers and clingers a good place to get a toehold.

I know it's a long shot, but if you are lucky enough to have a few actual ruins about the place, you are indeed fortunate. These crumbling walls make the ultimate in romantic enclosures. Many of the world's great gardens – Ninfa in Italy, Nymans in England, Eleutherian Mills in Pennsylvania, and Afton Villa in Louisiana – use old ruins as bones. In the late eighteenth century, English aristocrats spent fortunes building brand-new "ruins" for their gardens to create just the right feeling of pleasing melancholy. Of course, they also built picturesque hovels in their woods and hired antisocial types to dress poorly and live

The quintessential English walled garden, filled with spring bulbs and espaliered fruit trees. Cranborne Manor, England.

there as hermits in residence, which strikes me as excessive.

There should be a fairly level transitional area between the house and the garden (not necessarily paved, as I discovered, and even more not necessarily a deck) with some outdoor furniture for times when you want to behave as if you lived in California. In my corner of Vermont there are probably two or three evenings a year that approximate this climate, but it is universally accepted that all gardens should have this outside "room."

Where this area ends and the garden proper begins, a slight drop in height is a good idea, so that you can look down on your Eden and have the delusion that you are in control. Only a foot or two is necessary, which gives you a good excuse for putting in a couple of steps and, if it's appropriate and you are in an Italianate mood, a balustrade. I know this last touch is unlikely, but if we are imagining a formal sort of perfection, then why not? For most of us, a low hedge or bed of shrubs will serve the purpose. By the way, any temptation to use railroad ties for steps or changes in level should be scrupulously ignored. They are the work of the devil. They look fine under railroad tracks but inappropriate in a garden.

ABOVE AND OPPOSITE:
Japanese lanterns and 'Goldflame' honeysuckle adorn a fence, while the elegant clematis 'Huldine' scales an arbor.

FOLLOWING SPREAD:
At Stonecrop, near New York's Hudson River, steeple trellises are used to grow golden hop vines and purple climbing French beans.

THE LAST CATEGORY OF BONES UNDER DISCUSSION, and one of the most noteworthy because it lies well within the realm of possibility for any gardener, includes all those vertical, mostly wooden structures that give vines upward mobility. One of the most pleasing and characteristic things about gardens and houses of a century ago was the amount of vining, twining, climbing, and clambering that was going on. Vines were used extensively to soften the lines of buildings and blend them into their surroundings. Countless Victorian photographs show women in white shirtwaist dresses and men with beards amusing themselves on porches invariably smothered by a gargantuan grapevine or Dutchman's pipe. Often a gnarled wisteria vine as big around as a python is pictured reaching past clapboards and dark shutters to the

eaves, where it is ransacking the gutters. Places like the Alcotts' Orchard House or Frederick Law Olmsted's Fairsted (Victorians liked to give their properties impressive bucolic names) are shown buried in rampant tendriled greenery.

Trellises are the simplest of these supports, being basically two-dimensional and attached to walls. Arbors are a bit more elaborate and are often seen in the company of grapes. They have walls of latticework and provide shelter from the sun's glare as well as exercise for vines. Last but certainly not least is the pergola, a glorified and extended arbor of Mediterranean extraction that covers a path or walkway. It is made up of columns or posts that support an open framework of beams where interweaving vines form a roof of greenery. On a blazing August day a pergola is an oasis in the garden, filled with a cool, leaf-shaded, celadon-hued light.

Once a few vine-supporting bones are placed in the garden, a cornucopia of climbing plants awaits. Now vines that we always thought only the horticultural elite could grow are appearing in every suburban garden center. The hardy kiwi (*Actinidia arguta*), for instance, and *Hydrangea petiolaris*, a white-flowered slow starter that grows well in shade and after three or four years looks effective climbing up a wall or a large tree trunk. Clematis have become ubiquitous – even I can grow the large-flowered hybrid varieties like 'Nellie Mosher' and 'Henryi', which look like something out of the Brazilian rain forest. I've yet to attempt the more delicate species clematis, though, whose flowers are shaped like diminutive dangling trumpets. Perhaps some of the old-time dependables are more to your taste: hop vines, Thomas Jefferson's scarlet runner beans and Virginia creeper, 'Dropmore Scarlet' honeysuckle, wisteria, or azure morning glories.

A GARDEN WITHOUT BONES is all transient leaf and no enduring brick or stone. When summer is gone and Shakespeare's "yellow leaves, or none, or few, do hang upon those boughs which shake against the

ABOVE AND OPPOSITE:
*Wisteria blooming in unison
with crimson azaleas and
cloaking an ornate pergola
at Old Westbury Gardens
on Long Island.*

cold," it is reassuring to glance out the window and see the bones of the garden, no longer hidden, sturdy, well crafted, and beautiful in their own right. The stage is set, waiting for next spring's performance.

*A difficult, sloping garden
site is tamed with good
bones: a stairway, brick
balustrades, and a pair
of paved terraces with
contrasting formal pools.
Virginia House,
Richmond, Virginia.*

CHAPTER III

TREES & SHRUBS

Part of the afternoon had waned . . . the flood of summer light

had begun to ebb, the air had grown mellow, the shadows were

long upon the smooth, dense turf . . . The great still oaks and beeches

flung down a shade as dense as that of velvet curtains.

~ HENRY JAMES

IN 1888 CHESTER COOLEY set several lilac whips – two lavender and one white – a mock orange, a bridal wreath spirea, and a *Hydrangea paniculata* around his new farmhouse. He also planted nine maple saplings in an informal row in the front yard to shade the porch from the afternoon sun. Because I am the present inhabitant of "the old Cooley place," I feel greatly indebted to him for this largess and feel that we are oddly related by happenstance, horticultural rather than genealogical cousins, one century removed.

And now, how his children have grown! The lilacs have flourished, as they often do around old granite and lime-mortar foundations. They have swollen warty trunks as fat as good-sized apple trees, and their two-story telltale arching shapes authentically frame my old farmhouse. The other centenarians still unfailingly punctuate the passage of each summer with their bloom: the spirea its robin-chorused beginning, the mock orange its buzzing humid apex, and the hydrangea – with its greenish white pinnacles of flower burned pink by the first frost – its end.

Even more impressive are the maples, now lofty monarchs that form great arcs of green overhead. Not only do they provide perfect spots from

PAGE 48: *Azaleas and rhododendrons, Leonardslee, England.*

which to hang the hammock and the rope swing (both necessities of life, in my sybaritic opinion); but having reached a height of eighty feet and the broad arching form of mature specimens of their kind, they make vast pools of late afternoon shade for the porch and the garden. Not the deep gloomy variety under which nothing grows, but something infinitely better – a fluctuating leaf-filtered shade in which myriad small spots of sunlight shimmer and dance on the ground as the maples gently sway in the breeze. Without these giants, both my porch and my garden, which also faces west, would be nearly uninhabitable from four o'clock on – just the time that you want to savor either location, hoe or gin and tonic in hand.

BECAUSE TREES AND SHRUBS HAVE THIS KIND OF EFFECT on our lives, I have become an enthusiastic planter and transplanter, no doubt to a fault. My poor farm has been subjected to many bouts of tree mov-

ing and landscaping over the years in a sort of large-scale homage to Thomas Jefferson and his much-touted *ferme ornée.* This activity was even a source of some friction in my first marriage. One heated exchange comes immediately to mind. It was early May and the smell of fresh earth and rising sap was in the air. My wife had been after me, with plenty of justification, to plow up a piece of ground for some vegetables, especially tomato plants, as I recall. I was totally and no doubt infuriatingly absorbed in my Jeffersonian tree movings and had been ignoring her pleas. Tempers flared, and she said, "Richard, a tomato plant is just as important as a tree!" It was a perfectly valid statement, in a democratic, all-of-God's-creatures kind of way. Anyway, as we all know, such arguments aren't about the relative merits of trees and tomatoes at all; they're about empowerment, lack of communication, incompatible signs of the zodiac, and so forth. But I was younger then, hadn't read all those books, and was even less wise. I

ABOVE AND OPPOSITE:
A Vermont paper birch standing in a pool of Siberian irises and a grove of ornamental cherries at Upton House, England.

PREVIOUS SPREAD:
Venerable live oaks, the marker trees of the Deep South, are festooned with Spanish moss at Afton Villa, Louisiana.

ABOVE AND OPPOSITE:
Dogwoods, azaleas, and red camellias, Callaway Gardens, Georgia.

rose to the bait: "Well, then it's too bad old Chester Cooley didn't plant some nice tomato plants out in the front yard instead of all those lousy maples so we could be eating ourselves sick on heirloom tomatoes in the blinding sun!"(Naturally my retort has improved greatly in the recollection.) I'm happy to say that my ex-wife is now married to a man who grows a lot of tomatoes.

At that time I was still planting relatively modest trees, say three to four inches in diameter, digging them out of the ground by hand with a shovel and mattock and moving them to their ultimate destination with an ancient Ford 8N tractor and an old stone-boat (an antique contraption New England farmers used to haul stones out of their fields). However, as I have been tempted by ever larger and larger specimens, I have recently upgraded to a fifth-hand Mitsubishi excavator, affectionately known about the place as Old Mitsi. (I find in middle age that I have acquired some bad habits that I can ill afford, foremost among them collecting heavy machinery.)

Despite the size of the tree to be planted or the tools at hand, there are several rules of transplanting that are universal. I've learned the hard way that any nick or scarring of the bark is a potentially mortal wound, so I wrap the trunks in old rugs, tied with rope. Timing, as in most of life's endeavors, is everything. I have had good luck transplanting deciduous trees in autumn when the buds have formed and the leaves are just beginning to turn. This gives them a chance to grow new roots in the still warm earth and be better equipped the following spring when they leaf out. I usually move evergreens in May, though, because winter is especially hard on them, what with its wild fluctuations in temperature, lack of available moisture (which is locked up in ice), and the browning effects of wind and sun. The best favor you can do for them is to spray them thoroughly (except the roots) with a nontoxic polymer plant protectant, once when you plant them and again in the fall. Since I began doing this I have not lost a tree. With both evergreens and hardwoods, it's not a bad idea to cut some of

the growth out of the crown so that the depleted root system isn't over-taxed. Staking the tree with guy wires isn't as necessary as we have been led to believe, unless it is being planted in a very exposed spot or the root ball is too small to hold the tree upright. A normal amount of swaying caused by wind actually stimulates root growth.

EXPERIENCE HAS TAUGHT ME that trees are reassuringly resilient and tough hombres. As a case in point, I recall one very mild and busy fall when I put off transplanting until just after Thanksgiving. Neal, a jack-of-all-trades who is my usual accomplice in such misadventures, was helping me move some splendid hemlocks out of the woods when a cold front blew through, quickly followed by a blinding blizzard. It must have been a surreal scene, two grown men who should have known better planting trees in a foot of snow. The Mitsubishi slowly crawling along through a whiteout with a prize hemlock dangling from her bucket looked like a modern-day parody of the Currier and Ives scene "Bringing Home the Tree." Beneath the snow the ground was still soft, although the following morning it had turned to cement, locking every transplant in place. Of the dozen or so trees we moved that wild day, all but two made it, a convincing testament to their will to survive.

Trees, like children, grow up more quickly than we expect. I am always astounded by how a barren yard with a few spindly, insignificant sprigs suddenly seems crowded with full-limbed, rowdy giants. What did I think these saplings were going to turn into? When space is at a premium, there is a whole category of fastigiate trees such as cypress, pyramidal arborvitae, and Lombardy poplars to consider. They are slender, less rambunctious sorts with a sophisticated air about them – considerate trees that take up less room and throw relatively little shade. They make dramatic statements in the garden and have been used by gardeners to great effect since the Renaissance.

ABOVE: *White pine needles coated with frost add off-season interest to a Vermont garden.*

OPPOSITE: *Following the outburst of bloom, the fallen petals of flowering trees and shrubs provide an additional show.*

Some species of deciduous trees, such as oaks and beeches, retain their faded leaves throughout the winter, a subtle but welcome addition to the landscape.

MOST PEOPLE, MYSELF INCLUDED, plant shrubs for their appearance, but another desirable feature is fragrance. Those that I have scattered about the place – lilacs, *Philadelphus*, azaleas, daphnes, hydrangeas, viburnums – all have their own unique scent when in bloom. It's hard to describe the effect that fragrance has on the mind. Certainly there is a very strong element of nostalgia about it. Sight is immediate, of the moment, but fragrance is inexplicably mingled with memory. Oliver Wendell Holmes captured this mysterious power of fragrance – other times, other lives – far better than I can. He too was enamored of those damnable boxwoods:

> *They walked over the crackling leaves in the garden, between the lines of box, breathing its fragrance of eternity; for this is one of the odors which carry us out of time into the abysses of the unbeginning past; if we ever lived on another ball of stone than this, it must be that there was box growing on it.*

Azaleas have a striking spicy fragrance that is thoroughly invigorating. My very first morning in England, I found myself quite by accident at the entrance to Leonardslee, one of the premier azalea gardens in the world, at that moment in full candescent cry. After what I had just been through – frantic packing, the race to Logan, an all-night flight sitting next to a pathological talker (why me, Lord?), no sleep, dealing with Heathrow, and a terrorizing drive in a strange car on strange motorways on a strange side of the road – I was not at my best. The spectacle and especially the scent of that polychrome sea of azaleas, however, seemed to contain more caffeine than a double French espresso. Within minutes I was completely revived, quite euphoric in fact, and photographing for all I was worth.

Shrubs like spirea and weigela are subtler but equally distinctive. The scent of daphne is a touch cloying, perhaps, but it's one of those shrubs like box that you're not supposed to be able to grow north of Massachusetts, so I will forgive it any oversweetness. For some reason it thrives in one particular corner of my garden. It's even the variegated

OPPOSITE: Many azaleas are as prized for their singular fragrance as for their brilliant color. Leonardslee, England.

variety (*Daphne* x *burkwoodii* 'Carol Mackie'), which should be even more of a wimp than the basic green one. Another of its endearing habits is that if there are just a couple of Indian summer days in late November, it puts out another handful of blooms to lift my spirits before winter's inevitable siege. It's fine for Shakespeare to have felt that "at Christmas I no more desire a rose than wish a snow in May's new-fangled mirth," but he didn't live in Vermont – where winter is half the year and snow in May is a usual occurrence.

Hobblebush viburnum.

TREES AND SHRUBS MAY HAVE A REPUTATION for needing little care, but maintenance is a relative concept. They still need pruning, fertilizing (better too little than too much), shelter from snow sliding off the roof while they're young, and above all protection from predators. The worst offenders in my garden are the largest and smallest of the wondrous four-footed pageant that passes before my door: deer and mice. (I'm not counting the occasional moose or bear who wanders through, who hasn't yet shown any interest in my horticultural smorgasbord). The deer relish the yews, arborvitae, and especially my much coddled and prized Sargent weeping hemlocks – which I had assumed, what with Socrates and all, would be deadly poisonous. No such luck. The only answer is to hang a bar of Ivory soap in whatever shrub you want the deer to avoid. For some unfathomable reason, Ivory and only Ivory is ninety-nine and forty-four one-hundredths percent effective in this particular application. I usually don't get around to this chore until between Thanksgiving and Christmas, so it looks as if the garden has been decorated for the holiday season by some wise-guy elf who is strongly hinting that I need to take more baths.

The mice, if anything, are even more devious than the deer, tunneling under the snow in the dead of winter in search of my choicest shrubs to girdle. I foil them in the usual way, with several layers of hardware cloth placed around the stems and trunks. At first these lit-

tle devils seemed interested only in my dwarf lilac hedge, which they decimated for several years before I smartened up. They then switched to the two PJM rhododendrons by the porch, which – God knows why – I thought were immune. These flagrant beauties had replaced the infamous boxwoods. The following spring, after I watched them burst into raging purple bloom only to wilt, turn brown, and die, I realized that the mice had actually done me a favor. Those PJMs had always seemed a bit too garish, too relentlessly magenta, too downright Hawaiian for my taste. They had always brought to mind that Elinor Wylie line, "Down to the Puritan marrow of my bones, there is something in this richness that I hate." They were as immodest and flamboyant as bougainvillea. First the boxwoods, then the rhododendrons – I'm afraid I will never get it right.

Winkworth Arboretum,
Surrey, England.

Evergreen shrubs, well-manicured boxwood, and a weeping blue Atlas cedar, used for their contrasting textures and architectural qualities. Newton Vineyards, St. Helena, California.

CHAPTER IV

FAVORITE FLOWERS

Nearer the house was a portion given up entirely to flowers . . .
crammed together in an irregular square, where they bloomed in
half-wild profusion. There were rose bushes there and lavender and
rosemary and a bush apple-tree which bore little red and yellow
streaked apples in later summer, and Michaelmas daisies and
red-hot pokers and old-fashioned pompom dahlias in autumn and
peonies and pinks already budding.

~ FLORA THOMPSON

SOME PEOPLE WHO HAVE REACHED SUPERIOR LEVELS of gardening evolution have an annoying habit of dismissing flowers as somehow too common, too nouveau. They say how much more interesting they find the forms of plants, the subtle interplay of texture and leaf shapes, the rich variety of greens, and so on, as if to say, "Oh yes, we've done flowers but we've moved on from that." When flowers are permitted, they must be all one color, most notably white, in reverential obedience to Sissinghurst's masterpiece. I find this attitude particularly annoying because I would kill to have what they so casually dismiss, an overflowing multihued border crammed full of all the classic old-fashioned flowers. I heartily concur with Henry Mitchell, always the master of understatement, who wrote that "the idea is to grow at least a handful of the great flowers." (This from a man who once grew five hundred varieties of iris.)

These "great flowers" are mostly perennials, of course, and ironi-

PAGE 66: *Hollyhocks in their preferred setting, growing next to a weathered farmhouse wall.*

OPPOSITE: *Red and white valerian, blue campanula, and Iceland poppies blooming in a painterly mix at Monet's garden in Giverny, France. The artist once complained, "I am good for nothing but painting and gardening."*

cally, part of their charm lies in the very briefness of their visit. Each one's show lasts a week, perhaps two at most, then it's on to the next. This gives the gardener plenty of time for eager anticipation as the buds swell, just about enough time for fulfillment, and no time at all for ennui or surfeit. You will never hear a gardener say, "Enough of these peonies" or "I'm sick of looking at all these damned delphiniums," which is the basic problem with annuals. Marigolds and petunias just keep on wearing the same smile month after month. They're like used-car salesmen or television spokesmodels – lots of superficial charm but no sincerity.

In my garden there are several distinct waves of bloom, or peaks, that occur every year. The first is that great onslaught of mid-May, when any klutz of a gardener can get a good effect. All of nature's pent-up energy bursts forth; daffodils, tulips, forget-me-nots, creeping phlox, bleeding heart, candytuft, and alyssum run riot at just the moment that the crab apples and lilacs are in their full glory. In Vermont it is the best week of the year.

The garden is at its lushest, however, as June gives way to July, on the cusp of high summer, so to speak, when lupines, irises, nepeta, poppies, and peonies do their best to match the roses' florid display. Several weeks later lilies, delphiniums, campanulas, and *Veronica* 'Crater Lake Blue' take center stage, followed by August's hollyhocks, phlox, and rudbeckias. Eventually things wind down to the garden's swan song – "Oh, the days grow short when you reach September" – of coneflowers, aconitum, and asters. The English often talk about the difficulty of keeping their flower gardens "fully dressed" during the summer, as if their borders were given to impetuously tossing off their clothes in the heat, but I like a little rest between these outbreaks of bloom to tidy things up and attend to other tasks without being distracted by constant floral sartorial splendor – a chance to doze in the hammock or try to get the lawn mower to start.

We all have particular flowers that we are drawn to because of their look, their scent, their associations, or, in my case (I'm especially thinking of daylilies now), the fact that they will grow, even flour-

ish, in the face of my oversolicitousness, neglect, or just plain ignorance. Here are eight flowers that I have singled out as indispensable to my garden – my handful of personal favorites.

ABOVE AND OPPOSITE: *Daffodils growing in a Virginia bulb field, and gathered as cut flowers from the Sisters' Bulb Farm, Louisiana.*

Daffodil: Or, to be more correct, narcissus, as all of these trumpet-shaped yellow beauties fall into this category ("All daffodils are narcissus, but not all narcissus are daffodils," as one obnoxious know-it-all once informed me). The daffodil's color seems intentionally designed to make this the most cheerful flower at a time that we need cheering most: when the snow has left but the days lack real warmth and the landscape is still more brown than green. The whole idea with daffodils and narcissus is that they are supposed to look natural and nonchalant, haphazardly carpeting the ground in cheerfully nodding "drifts" as if they just happened that way, which they clearly did not. Gardeners spend a great deal of calculated effort and unnatural expense creating this natural look. Not surprisingly, my most successful drift occurred by accident, when I unceremoniously removed an old truck-tire planter from the front lawn with the tractor and dumped its contents along the edge of the stone wall that borders the back road. Apparently it was full of poet's narcissus (the genteel, nearly white ones with the delicate apricot-rimmed centers, *Narcissus poeticus*), because now there is a cheerful congregation of them in that spot every May.

Tulip: Highly domesticated flowers, the dogs and cats of the floral world, intimately associated with people and their gardens since the time of ruffle-collared Dutch burghers and their plump wives. Tulips have pure bright colors and a simple grace. They are straightforward flowers, with the exception of the parrot varieties, which suddenly appear in my garden each spring like overdressed, boisterous guests, preening and posturing and gesticulating in the wind and generally calling attention to themselves. Yet their extroverted beauty is so undeniable and unforgettable that their exhibitionism is immediately

forgiven. They are the life of the party and instantly transform a non-descript corner of the garden into a vibrant seventeenth-century Dutch still life.

Peony: The most flower for the least amount of effort; many live for more than a century, flourishing on benign neglect. There is something eminently nostalgic about them; they belong to a world of Victorian parlors, dark ornate furniture with marble tops, elderly ladies fussing over tea, and paintings by Fantin-Latour. Their big fat buds, always home to a half-dozen ants, signal the beginning of the really hot days.

I prefer the singles. They don't become a sodden, bedraggled mess after a shower and hardly need staking. However, I do grow some of the bomb types and doubles like 'Elizabeth Price' and 'Sarah Bernhardt' for cutting, because they look so opulent spilling out of an old pewter vase.

OPPOSITE AND ABOVE: *Hybrid tulips with their warm range of clarion colors dominate the spring borders at Old Westbury Gardens, New York.*

FOLLOWING SPREAD: *Peonies, the Mae West of perennials — sensuous, perfumed, and top-heavy.*

Iris: There are literally tens of thousands of bearded iris hybrids available in myriad pastel shades (Iris was the Greek goddess of the rainbow, after all), but I prefer the basic lavender ones that grow in sturdy clumps around every Vermont farmhouse of a certain vintage. Blue flag, the old-timers call them, but that name more commonly refers to the dark blue wild iris, *Iris versicolor*, that thrives in swamps. Other iris favorites of mine include dwarf varieties in deep maroon and yellow and pale blue that poke up between the terrace bricks and whose fan-shaped, spearlike leaves look neat and well mannered among all the chaos. My garden also has several clumps of Siberian iris 'Royal Herald', regal fleurs-de-lis that stand nearly four feet tall and whose great flock of blooms have the deep purple-blue incandescence of lapis lazuli. My one iris complaint is that the spent flowers don't fade very graciously; they're as ugly as last year's Christmas wreath. Frequent deadheading is a necessity.

ABOVE: *A lavender bearded iris underplanted with nepeta. Glebe House, Woodbury, Connecticut.*

OPPOSITE: *Oriental poppies.*

Poppy: Every garden needs a good shot of the oriental poppy's flaming orange color, like a dash of tabasco, to add a little fire to the stew and dispel any threat of border boredom. My problem is that I got a bit carried away (those seeds are awfully small, after all) and emptied the whole bottle. Their strident hue has always overpowered the garden for several weeks every June, resulting in visual heartburn. Last year I finally replaced most of them with the subtler salmon and watermelon pink varieties, keeping just enough of the originals to ward off any hint of dreariness. Poppies are the most fleeting of perennials – even their fuzzy gray-green foliage disappears soon after they bloom – but no other flower makes such a brilliant splash in the border, and once established they're fairly indestructible.

Delphinium: The monarch of the border, especially the Pacific Giant hybrids, which tower above every other flower and can even dwarf

the gardener. Their bloom is my garden's high point, both factually and figuratively – after their majestic fountains of bloom subside, it's all downhill.

I had beginner's luck with delphiniums: some very respectable plants the first summer and a dazzling display for several years following. Each summer after they bloomed, I'd cut them back to ground level and get another good show in September. Actually, it wasn't all luck. They like a cool climate – no problem there – and a steady diet of old cow manure, which I have up to my knees, often literally. An occasional dash of wood ashes is said to increase the brilliance of their colors, and my wood stove is always happy to oblige.

Now, of course, some damnable fungus or wilt has shown up (every time something is going too well in the garden, you can be sure Mother Nature, who I've learned is a sadistic, spiteful old crone, will intervene), and the only thing to do at this point is rip them out, burn them up, and start over. But delphiniums are like that. No one ever claimed they were easy. They are a lot of fuss and bother, what with staking (always a necessity), fertilizing, spraying, and periodic replacing. But what other plant repays the gardener with such a profound sense of accomplishment? I've been known to wander around in disbelief, muttering, "I can't believe I actually grew these things," when they are in their full splendor – great columns of bloom in shades of icy blue, deep gentian, royal purple, and that unique delphinium hue, an iridescent cerulean like some tropical butterfly's wing, that mirrors July's limitless sky.

Daylily: True no-care plants, just the opposite of delphiniums, and as tough as they come. Naturally, modern plant breeders have insisted on perfecting what was already perfect by messing with the chromosomes of the old-time daylily and have developed grotesque tetraploid varieties that look like they're on steroids. I prefer the unimproved variety, which has naturalized around an old cellar hole up my back road and formed bright orange swaths beneath the lichened gray walls. From time to time I have plundered these wild beds, and on one occasion, be-

OPPOSITE: Delphiniums are a recompense for enduring Vermont's arctic climate. They flourish in northern gardens.

ing distracted by some household emergency or other, I left a few plants tossed carelessly on the ground, where they languished throughout the winter. The following spring I happened upon their lifeless shriveled roots, took pity on them, and gave them a decent burial, and they have now risen from the dead and flourished. Daylilies have wills of iron. Lemon lilies are the first of the season, eager, friendly, bright yellow flowers. The more reserved and pale yellow 'Hyperion' lily is also very choice, tall, graceful, and strikingly fragrant. Its scent hits you like a wall of perfume on a humid August evening and pulls in every cecropia and luna moth for miles around.

Hollyhock: The flower of old New England homesteads, grown as much for what it epitomizes as for its bloom. Like the lilac, it belongs next to every cottage door. Of course I am referring to the singles, not those atrocious doubles that look like wads of crumpled-up crepe paper or worse and are actually called "powder puffs" in the seed catalogues. True venerable hollyhocks have delicious colors: claret, watermelon, peach, lemon, and a deep, dark, reddish black like bittersweet chocolate. These sovereigns of the dooryard rival delphiniums in stature, towering nine-foot spires with great knots of buds rising up the stalk that promise months of bloom – right into October if there isn't a killing frost.

PREVIOUS SPREAD:
The Mission House garden, Stockbridge, Massachusetts.

OPPOSITE: *A vase full of goldenrod and late summer favorites from my own garden.*

Hollyhocks are not without their problems, especially Japanese beetles and rust, which can severely defoliate them. They are also biennials, a condition I have always found complicated and troublesome in the abstract. In reality, however, once a clump is well established it self-seeds itself for eternity and might as well be a perennial.

GROWING A FEW OF THE TIME-HONORED STANDARDS connects us to the great mass of flower-loving humanity, both past and present. Believe me, I'm not immune to the siren song of this or that latest horticultural wonder at the nursery, and often return home with a carload of fancy new prospects, many of which are still in their green plastic pots when the snow begins to fall. My wife, Susan, chides me for having more of a green wallet than a green thumb. However, it is the old-fashioned perennials, the "handful of great flowers," with their time-proven beauty and wealth of associations, that are my favorites and grow in my garden, despite my misguided efforts, in a lush and pleasing confusion.

CHAPTER V

WATER *in the* GARDEN

*The greatest asset a garden can have — greater than four feet of
natural potting compost or a view of Mont Blanc — is a permanent
stream. Water wakes up a garden. It is the one element which is
biddable, to paint pictures and evoke moods at will.*

~ HUGH JOHNSON

IT IS AN UNQUESTIONED ASSUMPTION that every great
landscape or garden has a body of water in it. I was particularly struck by this truth when visiting Monticello
and Mount Vernon in quick succession. All Jefferson
was able to manage on his commanding but dry mountaintop site was a
little "fish pond" about the size of a wading pool, edged with bricks set on
end in a sawtooth pattern. Very disappointing. However, this man of
genius and collector of rare wines obviously knew that any water was better than none at all. Washington, in contrast, had the broadly flowing Po-
tomac rippling along beneath his veranda, an effect eminently more
satisfying (especially to a man whose career got a big boost from a timely
river crossing).

Decorators love to put mirrors in rooms to give them more depth
and sparkle; a bit of water, no matter what the size, has the same effect
in a garden. It adds an animated surface that ripples and catches the
changing lights and colors of the sky or, when still, the serene quality of
objects reflected. Even something as simple as a birdbath adds immea-
surably to a garden.

Water is another one of those garden features that provides interest

PAGE 86: *Reflections, Monet's garden.*

ABOVE AND OPPOSITE: *Swans and Siberian irises both enjoy getting their feet wet.*

when the blooming season is over or is yet to begin: falling leaves dappling the surface, the fernlike patterns of newly formed ice, the first trilling of the peepers, and the return of barn swallows skimming over the surface and snatching at insects.

In addition, small ponds and streams give gardeners the excuse or inspiration to grow another whole group of plants – the water lovers. These can be roughly divided into three personality types: the observers, the waders, and the swimmers.

The observers are the young matrons of the hydrophilic plant world, like the mothers of small toddlers who sit at the water's edge and visit among themselves while their children wreak havoc. They like to look at the water, enjoy being near it, but don't like to get more than their feet wet – plants like the primulas, marsh marigolds, and lady's slippers.

The waders are the raucous teenagers. They're rather show-offy, like to splash about and cause quite a commotion, but don't like to get

their hair wet – blue flag, the yellow *Iris pseudacorus*, and purple loosestrife (the wild invasive variety is about as popular with environmentalists as kudzu and dioxin, but undeniably beautiful).

The swimmers are the serious water-sports types – plants that really like to get in the water and swim. They aren't afraid to go out where it's over their head – the waterlilies, lotuses, and water hawthorn.

PONDS ALWAYS LOOK ESPECIALLY PICTURESQUE if a few waterfowl are paddling about. However, you need a rather large body of water to keep these birds safely. They need a means of escape so that foxes can't behead them. And while swans and ducks are very appealing in the abstract, unless you have a good-size pond they really foul their nest, if you know what I mean. Also, the large Peking ducks of Chinese restaurant fame, who spend a lot of their time parading around on the grass, are constantly leaving a trail of white feathers in their wake,

OPPOSITE AND ABOVE: *Waterlilies and purple loosestrife are two aquatics that grow with little effort. In fact, the latter is considered a nuisance because of its aggressive nature, but noninvasive cultivars are available for the gardener.*

The tranquil effects of water in the garden were never more beautifully realized than at Courance, a chateau built at the edge of France's Fontainbleau forest.

The Fountain of Latona and the frogs, Versailles, France.

so that your lawn looks like the scene of some especially violent pillow fight. When I kept a few of these fat waddlers I was always picking up after them. I even went so far as to order one of those lawn sweeper contraptions from Sears, Roebuck, the Craftsman Deluxe Model, which (after I finally managed to assemble the thing) I would push around and use compulsively to gather up all that errant down. This activity took place only when I was sure none of the neighbors were looking.

EARLY GARDEN WATER FEATURES were primarily formal and only affordable by the aristocracy. The elaborate fountains and waterworks at palaces like Villa d'Este and Versailles were really the first theme parks – built for royal amusement and practical jokes. Kings, noblemen, and even cardinals, like naughty boys with squirt guns, liked nothing better than seeing their guests, especially the ladies, getting soaked unexpectedly by trick fountains. The efforts of artisans and engineers to create and power all of those wondrous water staircases, triple-tiered fountains, and regurgitating nymphs and satyrs were nothing short of miraculous. Even now the French government can afford to fire up Versailles's fountains only once or twice a week. Statuary and water have always been a surefire combination; there is something fundamentally satisfying about all those gods and goddesses frolicking in the most basic life-sustaining element.

The sort of water feature that I had in mind for my garden was infinitely more plebeian and utilitarian but also Gallic in inspiration. It was the result of a memorable midday meal in Aix-en-Provence, eaten at a small outdoor café next to an ancient courtyard fountain. The hot sun, the brilliant blue sky and ochre buildings, the welcome shade of a plane tree, the pleasant hum of foreign conversation, the delectable cassoulet, and above all the pleasantly mesmerizing sound of the cool mountain water plashing into that ancient stone trough made this, for me, the quintessential South of France experience. I have since been told that it was all a matter of negative ions, those subatomic particles that are given off by water in motion and have a salubrious effect on the human psyche. Apparently they are the reason it feels so good to walk along the beach or look at a waterfall or sit by a stream. In fact, I had so many negative ions and positive sips of wine that afternoon that soon after the meal I bought two hundred pounds of copper pots and pans from a street vendor for a song, and was feeling very self-satisfied until I realized that I couldn't exactly drive them home to Vermont. But I digress.

A decorative stone bridge and man-made lake at Stourhead, Wiltshire, England.

Naturally I wanted to duplicate this negative-ion-producing wonder in my garden, but with more of a rural New England feeling, ideally with an old granite farmyard trough like one I had seen at Sturbridge Village — a massive thing covered with moss and lichens but worn smooth around the rim by a century or two of cows' necks rubbing against it, slightly cracked in one spot and kept together with a giant wrought-iron staple. I searched and searched to no avail and finally decided to make my own out of a special concrete mixture I had read about in *Horticulture* magazine. This material was supposed to be a dead ringer for antique Cotswold limestone once it had mellowed a bit. My one misgiving was that the magazine article dealt with a birdbath-size effort, whereas I was envisioning something along the lines of a very large rectangular bathtub. Neal set to work building the forms out of plywood, and we made allowances for plenty of rebar and outside reinforcement.

ABOVE AND OPPOSITE:
A formal raised pool and rose-tinged waterlilies at Old Westbury Gardens.

The mixture called for equal parts cement mix, perlite, and peat moss. Just to be on the safe side, we also planned to throw in some fiberglass filaments for additional strength. A cement mixer was rented, all the ingredients were assembled, and we set to work – perhaps a little too late in the afternoon, in hindsight. It soon became evident that something was going awry with the peat moss part of the project. We kept dumping it into the form, where it completely vanished. Cries of "More peat moss, more peat moss" echoed among the green hillsides. Little did we realize that owing to some adverse law of displacement we no doubt failed to learn in high school science class, all the peat moss was lying on the bottom and everything else was sitting on top (I would have thought it would be the other way around). We kept mixing and shoveling and cursing, and by the halfway point we had run out of the stuff. After scavenging the neighborhood, we came up with one miserable mildewed bag, which we eked out through the remainder of the job. The task was finally finished in the dark, by flashlight, and I retired exhausted, discouraged, and filled with foreboding at what daylight and the removal of the forms would reveal. Well, every bag of peat moss has a silver lining, or whatever, because the haphazard mixture of that ingredient had resulted in the most beautiful striated effect. Our cement trough looked exactly like some kind of ancient sedimentary rock. For the rest of the morning, while it was still green, I was Michelangelo working away with trowels and chisels and a piece of old chain, sculpting, beating, goug-

ing, and – for the final touch – smoothing the rim where the cows' necks had rubbed for a century or two. Barely a week later a neighbor dropped by and exclaimed, "Where did you get that magnificent old stone trough?" I suspect Susan bribed him.

Now that such a convincing-looking receptacle was in place, I definitely wanted the water flowing into it to be "real" and not recirculated around and around by some electrical pump. I didn't want to be like the man whose children said to me, "We knew company was coming because Dad turned on the waterfall." Even though such pumps use little electricity and are virtually silent, there is still this gnawing sense of artificiality to them. So I tapped into an old spring that was fortuitously located in an uphill swampy area behind the house. It dutifully provided the necessary gravity feed, but the water does have a slightly brownish cast and a slightly foul gassy odor when August's dog days are upon us. On the plus side, it is filled with nutrients for the moss and lichens that have already begun to mellow the trough's superbly crafted surface.

This source also contains plenty of insect life and mosquito larvae to feed the resident goldfish, who grow fat without ever being fed by me. These piscatorial inhabitants – a good deal more orange than gold – are actually a form of small carp called comets. They are quite entertaining and even have rudimentary personalities, floating to the top when called, where they look at you with their fishy eyes and make amusing sucking sounds at the water's surface. My stepdaughter has given them all names, of course. The only one I can remember is Sparkle-lips.

Perfecting the sound of the water as it trickles into the trough is a very tricky business indeed. It takes many attempts to tune this instrument properly, to get just the right sibilance, the ideal timbre. You don't want it to sound like a bathtub about to overflow or a truckdriver relieving himself after a long haul. I have often heard tales while photographing city gardeners' fountains of irate neighbors complaining that the noise was driving them crazy – horror stories of protracted bitter feuds or quagmires of acrimonious litigation.

Fortunately, I have no neighbors within earshot of my mellifluous creation. And I don't mind telling you, with what I hope is uncharacteristic smugness, that it is an unqualified triumph. It has even provided an unforeseen fringe benefit. The bright red circular handle on the shut-off valve (hidden behind the wall) has proven irresistible to hummingbirds. When they get tired of trying to sip its nonexistent nectar, they often alight on the edge of the trough to pause for a brief drink and to ponder the mysteries of this strange iron flower.

Now, sitting in the garden's summer dusk, like Whitman, "I lean and loaf at my ease," listening to the faint rustle of bird wings, the rattle of a dragonfly, the children's laughter as they pursue their "pet" frog, or the cat's purr as he reclines on the trough's edge eyeing Sparkle-lips' lazy piscine movements – and mingled with it all the gentle trickle of water, filling the evening air with blissful negative ions and primordial liquid music.

ABOVE: *Villa Mansi, Tuscany, Italy.*

FOLLOWING SPREAD: *A naturalistic and artfully contrived pool – well within the scope of any diligent gardener. The Victory Garden, Lexington, Massachusetts.*

CHAPTER VI

ORNAMENT

But still of dress and ornament beware;

And hide each formal trace of art with care:

Let clust'ring ivy o'er its sides be spread,

And moss and weeds grow scattered o'er its head.

~ RICHARD PAYNE KNIGHT

*I*T MAY BE DIFFICULT TO GROW the fabled Tibetan blue poppy, but it is far more difficult to include ornament in the garden successfully. All those nonblooming flourishes and embellishing touches that are meant to add drama, refinement, or charm are fraught with peril. Our modern sensibility tends to view anything with purely decorative purpose as highly suspect. Form must follow function, we are told, and if there is no useful function other than pleasing the eye, well, then what?

Statues are especially tough. It is almost impossible to place one in a garden without its appearing odd, cloying, or ludicrous. To begin with, all the good garden sculptors died a hundred years ago. In the past the idea behind such statuary was to create idealized human and animal forms to inhabit an idealized Eden – our gardens. The results were graceful and beautifully proportioned Venuses and Adonises, sleek lions and faithful canines, gleeful cherubs, wondrous winged angels, fierce griffins, and other assorted miraculous mythological beings. Today, extremely few of us could afford sculpture for our gardens by a contemporary master, and I doubt many of us would want some giant kinetic thing with blades rattling ominously in the landscape, or a blinding polished stainless

PAGE 102: *Afton Villa, Lousiana.*

ABOVE AND OPPOSITE: *Statues of beasts, both domesticated and wild, were popular features in seventeenth-century gardens. Courance, France.*

steel assemblage that looks like two heating ducts mating. These do well on the grounds of museums, but it takes a masterwork of modern domestic architecture to stand up to them. At the opposite extreme are all the whirling Sylvesters and Tweety Birds, peeing urchins and bending-over ladies fashioned from painted plywood and made to be stuck in the ground – quite a cottage industry in my rural backwater of New England. I own a particularly tasteless collection of these, which I stick in the lawn and garden from time to time to appall my daughters and to discourage anyone who might be in the neighborhood handing out religious tracts.

I did take one stab at putting a real statue in my garden, a nearly life-size granite Chinese temple carving of a very beguiling and ancient-looking maiden which I bought on the spur of the moment in a Boston antiques store. I thought she was going to be a perfect piece of sculpture for the garden – very classy, all blackened and lichen-encrusted and weighing about as much as a pickup truck. But when I got her home, she didn't look very happy or (you would think I would have learned this lesson by now) very at home in her plain Yankee surroundings. I also grew somewhat suspicious when I spied what appeared to be her twin, or at least her half-sister, in a junk shop somewhere in the wilds of Maine. Perhaps forging Asian antiquities is also a cottage industry in these parts. Now she's taken up residence in the house, where she appears more contented and spends her days looking out a window at the garden in her inscrutable Down East way.

No, the garden sculpture I am still searching for has to be more rural and bucolic in flavor, a shepherd or shepherdess or perhaps even a swain. We don't hear much about swains these days, and I think they may be ready for a comeback. According to my dictionary they are male rustic peasants, people rather like myself, who toil in the good earth on occasion but who, unlike myself or anyone else I know, are prone to outbursts of morris dancing and flute playing and the like. They are uninhibited, carefree, and definitely know how to have a good time. An-

other strong contender would be a large gray-green sheep or cow from an old weathervane, but such things cost as much as a whole herd of the real ones and are apt to wander. Statues are tough.

BROKEN BITS OF ARCHITECTURE, PIECES OF COLUMNS, capitals, and friezes, are much less of a challenge; they always look good in gardens – it's that ruins thing again. Any bit of old marble or granite with ivy clambering over it seems to work fine. It should be half concealed, and the more mysterious and intriguing, the better – something to raise the hairs on the back of your neck slightly and give your thoughts a pleasantly spooky or melancholy turn. On several occasions I have even seen and admired old tombstones placed in gardens but haven't dared ask how they got there. People are fond of burying much-beloved pets in a corner of the garden, but these stones were definitely for their masters. Once in a garden on the coast of Connecticut I stumbled across a large half-buried ship's bell, which gave the place an eerie shipwrecked feeling and tied in nicely with the buoys clanging in the fog offshore. Any similar use of ornament that adds mood and romance, that lifts the garden from the usual conventionality, should be encouraged.

Clay flower pots and other plant containers that don't look like plastic are the easiest and least pretentious forms of garden ornament. Every gardener should have a good collection of these in various shapes and sizes, all nicely streaked with the green patina they acquire with age and use. A plant that looks insignificant or out of place in the ground can benefit greatly from the added status of having its own pot.

Potted plants are like punctuation marks in the garden, adding emphasis or closure to various horticultural passages. They can be used to define areas like pathways and openings that might otherwise seem a bit vague. Every spring I enjoyably waste a lot of time messing around with pots and geraniums, filling holes in the garden or attempting just the right touch of balance or hint of formality where necessary. Geraniums are a godsend, instantly pepping up a lackluster effect. I also plant invasive things that I like but want to keep in check, like *Artemisia*

PREVIOUS SPREAD:
Cherubic dancers and musicians entertain the azaleas and live oaks at Afton Villa.

OPPOSITE:
Architectural fragments used as garden ornament, Hever Castle, Kent, England.

OPPOSITE:

The ancient Italianate pot adds as much to the picture as the hibiscus it holds. Villa Vizcaya, Miami, Florida.

'Silver King', in some of my larger pots. Artemisia has a nice Mediterranean feeling when treated this way. Actually, when I get discouraged by some particularly uncooperative plants in the garden and am feeling mean and vindictive, I fantasize about freeing these aggressive types – the artemisias, aegopodiums, and Japanese anemones – from their clay confines and setting them loose amid all those ingrates and prima donnas to plunder and pillage to their heart's content. I could just sit back without a gardening care in the world, enjoy the carnage, and see which one wins. I could even write one of those gardening books with a catchy title like *The Invasive Gardener* – but again I am straying from the subject at hand.

Part of the reason that pots work so well as garden decoration is that they certainly have a utilitarian as well as an ornamental value. If they have something growing in them, they can't appear entirely frivolous. The same can be said for all of the antique gardening paraphernalia that gardeners collect and like to strew about the garden casually for that much sought-after look of tasteful neglect: slightly dented, verdigris-stained watering cans with burnished copper roses, gardening tools of a certain age and wooden wheelbarrows in old blue paint, antique brass nozzles, glazed edging tiles, and elaborate Victorian plant markers and the like. I wish there were a good explanation for why these older examples of gardening tools and accouterments are so beautiful and all their modern counterparts at the hardware store are so ugly.

BENCHES ARE ANOTHER VERY POPULAR FORM of garden ornament. I put them in this decorative category because they are often very handsome – intricate cast-iron versions made like intertwining ferns or elegant teak concoctions like the celebrated Lutyens model – but few are actually home to the human posterior. It's hard for gardeners to sit still in their gardens; they fidget like six-year-olds. They immediately spot something that needs attending to. It eats at them, and they can't rest until it's corrected. It is really more the idea of sitting and relaxing that these benches provide, the invitation. The mere sight of a deftly positioned bench – well shaded and with a fine prospect – gives the

*Old flower pots, tools,
and watering cans exhibit
a well-crafted, utilitarian
beauty.*

mind that what-a-perfect-spot-to-while-away-the-afternoon-with-a-good-book kind of thought. Just the possibility offers a refreshing and pleasing moment that perpetuates the universally held illusion that gardens are for relaxation.

More extreme examples of leisure-conjuring ornament are all those gingerbread gazebos and elaborate summer houses that sprang up in gardens a century ago. Retreats, I believe they were called, though now they are more often havens for spiders and swallows than for the gentry taking tea. I used to think they were pretty silly but confess to a growing fondness for these whimsical structures, and I have actually drawn up plans for one. Mine would be a fairly simple hexagonal affair with an elegant bell-shaped roof based on an original example that has somehow survived, though at a rakish angle, in a tangle of lilacs behind a neighbor's farmhouse. All gazebos should have lattice arches on the sides, as this one does. They should contain benches or seats that are actually comfortable to sit in and be enveloped in clematis and climbing roses – the perfect spot to ignore the telephone, wait out a shower, or escape from visiting relatives' obnoxious children. I suspect my gazebo will remain unbuilt, however, because judging from past experience, the idea of it is much more enjoyable than the actuality. Once it was finished I would undoubtedly wish it were about seven feet more to the right or whatever. And instead of encouraging the aforementioned soothing activities, it would more likely be used as a spot to think

ABOVE: *The vegetable garden summer house at Jefferson's Monticello, Charlottesville, Virginia.*

OPPOSITE: *An ornate Victorian bench can be glimpsed through conservatory doors, Villa Vizcaya.*

up the next exhausting, noisy, and labor-intensive project designed to promote peaceful repose. For truth be known, most of the enjoyment in these fanciful outdoor structures is in the creating and not in the reposing.

GARDEN ORNAMENT SHOULD BE LIKE A DESSERT. It should be a delightful finish to the horticultural feast but not the main course itself. If it is too prevalent, it makes us feel glutted. If it is too sweet and cloying, it sets our teeth on edge. But no ornament at all is just as bad; the garden appears lifeless and lacking, and we are left with a gnawing sense of disappointment. Maybe I'll move that Chinese maiden back outside.

On the grounds of Barrett House in New Ipswich, New Hampshire, a Gothic Revival summer house crowns a terraced hillside. The allee of sugar maples was set out in the early nineteenth century.

CHAPTER VII

ROSES

There is probably no inanimate object in the world more
beautiful than a delicately tinted Rose. There is certainly nothing
else which combines such beauty of form and color with such
exquisite delicacy of texture and such delicious perfume . . . The
charm seems to me to lie, in great part, in the fine silky texture of
the petals and in their translucency . . . It is the charm which it
shares with every beautiful thing which is "hidden yet half revealed."

~ GEORGE COCHRAN LAMBDIN

OF ALL THE GARDEN FLOWERS, the rose is the most laden with sentiment. It is the flower most subjected to embarrassing similes by besotted lover, the one most touted in verse. Poets from Milton to T. S. Eliot have leaned heavily on the rose. It is the rose's lush blooms that most often grace vases in old, opulently framed paintings. It is the flower most often given by all of us to beg favor or forgiveness.

Perhaps because of this weighty emotional load, roses are intimidating to the novice. Certainly I find them so. They are also bewildering in their sheer numbers and highly varying personalities. The thousands of roses available to today's gardener are bred from a far-flung and complex lineage of species that include the musk and moss roses, the ancient *Rosa gallica* – known since Roman times as the apothecary's rose – the damasks, albas, and eglantines, the lavish cabbage roses, whose heavy blooms droop languidly from their canes, and finally the fabled *Rosa*

chinensis and *Rosa gigantea,* brought from China by acquisitive English merchantmen at the close of the eighteenth century. From this exotic and heady mix were bred the hybrid tea roses, which are said to smell like a well-brewed cup of tea – an odd though appealing comparison – and the floribundas.

Living as I do just below the Arctic Circle, I can't grow the quintessential florist's roses – those perfectly formed, languorously unfurling, long-stemmed sirens that come to mind when people think of Valentine's Day or cosmetic ads in glossy magazines. Those florabundas and hybrid teas are the temperamental divas of the rose world and demand as much attention to their living quarters, feeding, and medication as the most exasperating soprano. To begin with, they like to have separate gardens all to themselves – gardens that are usually laid out in unimaginative formal beds that smell more of malathion and tetradifon than roses. When these pampered primas are not performing (one of their great appeals is that they do bloom often), they have a gangly, awkward look that is disappointing at best. And because no other flowers are allowed to take up the slack, the show is over until the next year.

Some rose gardens, however, don't appear overly exclusive or completely sterile out of season. Beatrix Farrand, for instance, laid out a charming rose garden at Dumbarton Oaks in Georgetown. I think it actually looks its best under a light snowfall.

The French have always had a thing for roses, and have created formal gardens for that flower with consummate flair. Bagatelle and L'Hay-les-Roses, both on the outskirts of Paris, come immediately to mind. The Empress Josephine, inspired in part by her own middle name, which happened to be Rose (the names given to offspring often have powerful and unforeseen consequences), created one of the first formal rose gardens at Malmaison. She had both the good taste and the good luck to commission Pierre Joseph Redouté to paint her prize specimens, for which we can all be grateful.

ABOVE: *The white miniature rose 'Cinderella' and the flamboyant 'Joseph's Coat' blooming in the parterre garden at Newton Vineyards.*

OPPOSITE: *Rose arbor, Villandry, France.*

PAGE 122: *The Bagatelle rose garden, Paris.*

MY ROSES ARE LESS REFINED, far scruffier and far more cantankerous than anything that might have tempted Empress Josephine or Redouté. I am partial to roses that like to mingle and join in the fray: the shrubs, climbers, and ramblers. Their entire aspect is humbler and more cottagelike; their ungainly exuberance lends itself to this effect. These roses look especially good mixed with old-fashioned lavender and white flowers like nepeta, campanula, feverfew, and delphinium.

True climbing roses deserve an arch to embellish. Their lengthy canes have an upward, gently curving nature that easily conforms to this type of support. They are not vines, however, and do need some assistance – a surreptitious bit of twine here and there keeps them securely in place. Ramblers are even more flexible and long-caned; they are exceedingly relaxed and like a wall or a fence to lounge on or drape over.

Only a few roses have done well in my garden, all very common and unexciting to a true rose aficionado but much appreciated by me for their generous, untemperamental nature. There is a large clump of *Rosa rubrifolia*, with its distinctive smoky reddish foliage and small star-shaped pink flowers. I first saw this rose featured in the main border at Hidcote, so growing it makes me feel very accomplished and worldly, even though all I've ever done is poke the original shoots into the ground and then ignore them. Apparently it thrives on neglect. 'Pink Grootendorst' is another very tough and trouble-free cultivar, featuring numerous clusters of carnation-like flowers in an unusual warm pink shade. It blooms repeatedly, right through the first few frosts. Then there is 'Therèse Bugnet', a very feminine and Gallic rose, as the name implies, with soft refined foliage, tiny though numerous thorns, and delicate Old World–looking blooms.

'William Baffin', one of the Canadian Explorer series, is the only real climber that reliably blooms for me with no winter protection. Absolutely none. Some people in this latitude go to absurd lengths to grow less hardy climbers like 'Blaze', stripping the canes off their supports each fall, then laying them out along the ground and encasing them

in an elaborate cocoon of mulch and plastic to winter over, only to reverse the whole process the following spring. I'm not that much of a fanatic. Besides, I like the look of 'William Baffin' better – very informal and cheerful.

ABOVE: *A carmine-colored climber on a weathered Nantucket wall.*

OPPOSITE: *The white vintage rose 'Madame Alfred Carrière' properly engulfs an arch in a Massachusetts seaside garden.*

MY FAVORITE ROSE, however, will have to remain unnamed. Like the truck-tire planter, the geriatric draft horse, and the leaking basement, it came with the place, and I haven't a clue what it is. In fact, I prefer it that way. Flowers, like people, are often more interesting when their past is shrouded in mystery. It grows in rank profusion at the edge of the pasture in front of my house. I assume it was planted there in the 1880s, along with the maples and lilacs. At any rate, it is certainly an old-fashioned variety of questionable though undeniably hardy parentage.

This rose lacks many of the attributes of the modern hybrids. It blooms only once, and it doesn't die well. As the blossoms fade to brown, they hang on the branches tenaciously, like ticks on a dog. But for the last week of June and the first week of July it does what every rose is supposed to do, bursting into unabashed bloom and filling the air with that unmistakable and memorable rose scent.

When I first saw this rugged specimen, I was impressed by its vigor and especially its profuse thorns. As rapierlike and skin-rending as a cat's claws, they held the most gluttonous and dimwitted Holstein at bay. But something was lacking, that essence of old-fashioned cottage roseness, that feeling of unbridled, rampant, overrunning engulfment. This kind of rose looks its best only when it is on the attack, so to speak. It needed a victim, and I was only too happy to oblige. No, I'm not referring to myself, though I was wounded in the process. I am speaking of an authentic-looking rail fence, which Neal and I laboriously split from native cedar and snaked through this fierce jungle – with some minor bloodletting and major cursing. A bluebird house nailed onto the tallest fence post completed the picture, and within a

OPPOSITE: Rosa gallica officinalis, *the ancient "red rose of Lancaster," blooms in the William Paca colonial garden, Annapolis, Maryland.*

year my mystery rose had properly engulfed these offerings, leaving just enough glimpses of cedar rail and bird domesticity (tree swallows, naturally, not bluebirds) to tantalize and beguile. Now this conquering rose of yesteryear looks as it should.

This to me is the essence of roseness. Roses should overwhelm, engulf, nearly suffocate. A halfhearted one is an embarrassment to its kind as well as its keeper. If a rose looks spindly, is suffering from low self-esteem, bears but a few sad, limp blooms, tear it out and start over. Show no mercy. Roses should be effusive. Roses should smother their immediate surroundings with bloom and with fragrance. That is their life's calling. That is their destiny. That and graciously bearing the sentimental weight we place on their thorny, arching canes.

CHAPTER VIII

WOODLAND & MEADOW

I believe in the forest, and in the meadow, and in the night
in which the corn grows.

~ HENRY DAVID THOREAU

I N AN IDEAL SITUATION, forest and meadowland form the backdrop for the garden proper and make a graceful transition from the cultivated to the wild. These marginal areas are often the most pleasing part of the overall scheme – less forced, out of the horticultural spotlight, but filled with a quiet beauty that is the perfect complement to the more flagrant showiness of perennial borders, cascading roses, and sparkling fountains.

The quality of "edge" in nature, those places at the outer fringe of the forest that are particularly attractive to wildlife, is very important. Woodland and meadow edges to the garden have much the same feeling of energy and life. The interplay of sunlight and shadow, open clearing and leafy grove promotes a feeling of well-being that is akin to the salutary effects of running water.

The most appealing woodland and meadow gardens are those that seem natural but are in fact an "improved," idealized, and humanized form of nature. This is not as easy as it sounds, for it is often more difficult to attempt the subtle and unaffectedly natural than the straightforward and blatantly formal – "so that it looks less as if it had been planned than as if it might have come naturally" was how Gertrude Jekyll put it. This form of gardening is a particularly English invention that began

PAGE 134: *Double trillium and purple and white* Phlox divaricata *spill over a hillside at the Redfield wildflower garden in eastern Connecticut.*

ABOVE AND OPPOSITE: *Ornamental ferns and hostas as well as delicately colored foxgloves prefer the open shade of a wooded garden.*

in the late 1700s with the romantic parkland movement based on the pastoral landscape paintings of Claude and Poussin. One hundred years later, Jekyll and William Robinson were creating less aristocratic and more intimate "wild gardens," which were the prototypes of today's woodland and meadow gardens. The English have always had this affinity for the pastoral and wooded landscape, and it can be argued that much of their countryside is basically one huge garden. It is said that Eskimos have a hundred different words for describing snow, and it seems as if the English have about that many for describing what in this country we simply categorize as woods or fields. They have copses and spinneys, fens and hedgerows, wolds and wealds, brakes and chases, and so on. It all sounds very poetic and Ye-Olden. Whatever the nomenclature, gardens that emulate these seminatural areas make good sense in America, where the vast majority of our house lots are carved out of second-growth forest or abandoned open farmland. Of-

ten substantial remnants of woodland or meadow are already in place, just begging for a little "improvement."

Woodland gardening often begins as a subtractive process. Like sculpting or editing, it is an art of judicious removal. Low limbs, crowded or sickly trees, severe leaners, blowdowns, and trees that are permanently bent low by winter snow need to be disposed of, thereby opening up areas for that enticing dappled wood and glade effect. In subtracting, we want to bring the best features of the woodland into sharper focus – to make a virtue out of not seeing the forest for the trees. Unlike the usual gardening experience, in which we plant pathetic little sprigs of things and try to imagine what they will look like when and if they ever reach full growth, woodland gardening, at least as I have practiced it, requires that we imagine what the effect will be when something very large is eliminated. "Chainsaw gardening" is what I've come to call it, and it's not for the dainty or the indecisive. Once a fullgrown tree is lying on the ground, there's no putting it back, at least in our lifetime.

ABOVE AND OPPOSITE:
Crown vetch, sensitive fern, and wild phlox carpet a woodland garden.

PREVIOUS SPREAD:
A meadow garden seeded with annual cornflowers and field poppies at Glencoe in eastern Pennsylvania.

A woodland garden should look healthy, cared for, tended, gently guided. It should have that well-kempt look, like a Swiss beech woods where the local villagers have gathered up all the fallen limbs and underbrush for firewood. Trees look nobler when they have room to breathe. Imagine Sherwood Forest or the sort of woodland that James Fenimore Cooper was fond of describing:

The trees were tall, large, and so free from under-brush, that they resembled vast columns, irregularly scattered, upholding a dome of leaves. Although they stood tolerably close together, for their ages and size, the eye could penetrate to considerable distances; and bodies of men, even, might have engaged beneath their cover, with concert and intelligence.

The amount of filtered sunlight that is allowed in these more open areas is critical. The right amount encourages the spread of foam-

The seasonal coloration of leaves in both spring and autumn can rival the perennial border for putting on a show.

flowers, dogtooth violets, Solomon's seal, and other choice native plants. Too much sun and eager raspberries take over or, worse still, their more vicious cousins – killer blackberries studded with thorns like tiger's claws (in late August their fruit is much appreciated, however). Depending on soil type and climate, various shade-tolerant flowering shrubs and trees can be introduced to provide an understory of bloom: viburnums, azaleas, kalmia dogwood, and redbud (a tree that has a decidedly southern accent but will grow in milder parts of the north; the most magnificent specimen I have seen was growing in Connecticut).

Of course the look you want on the forest floor proper is the much-celebrated carpet-of-flowers effect, sheets of bloom all very natural and haphazard-looking: wild blue phlox, trilliums, lilies-of-the-valley, hepaticas, violets, perhaps even a few clumps of lady's slippers. However, these are all spring-flowering, so after their show subsides you need

some middle and late bloomers coming along, like foxgloves, Turk's cap lilies, and astilbes.

Ferns look especially good in shady areas of woodland gardens. The hay-scented variety is excellent both for its soft feathery appearance and the aroma it gives off when crushed in the hand. It tolerates a good deal of sun and is less fussy about being damp than most of its kin. I've transplanted a great many ostrich ferns, which are the most regal and showy of the genus, often reaching a height of five feet. They are also the ferns that produce edible fiddleheads in late May, just when the morel mushrooms are appearing. The combination of the two makes a memorable feast.

A MEADOW IS THE OBVIOUS ANSWER for marginal garden areas devoid of trees. Meadows conjure up all those arcadian images of misty green vales and fine flowery meads that lurk in our collective subcon-

scious, the sort of places where Botticelli goddesses like to frolic or Manet's bohemians have their *dejeuner sur l'herbe.*

The beauty of meadow gardening is that often relatively poor soil yields the best results. I have a meadow garden that partially created itself after I cut some Norway pine that had been planted in a played-out field during the Depression. (Vermont farmers were told these trees would grow into a cash crop that would save the farm, but Norway pine turned out to be pretty sorry lumber.) After the trees and stumps were removed, this fallow ground seeded itself from the surrounding countryside with native wildflowers – ox-eye daisies, Indian paintbrush, blue-eyed grass, yellow cinquefoil, and purple asters – which I then augmented with some of the more rugged garden annuals and perennials. Lupines do especially well in meadows; poppies also. Bachelor buttons, daisies, daylilies, rudbeckias, even peonies can flourish – anything that is durable and enthusiastic enough to compete with the native plants and grasses.

This kind of garden does not usually happen entirely on its own, however, and demands more maintenance than its casual laissez-faire appearance would imply. After yanking out brambles, nettles, burdock, and any other particularly noxious weeds, the gardener has to either plow under the whole area and seed it with the proper mix or dig up and sow many small patches in the hope that they will spread over the remainder. If all goes according to plan and a lush pastoral tangle of bright flowers and waving grasses is the result, an annual mowing is essential for carrying the full effect forward from year to year. Without its yearly shearing, a meadow soon becomes choked with brush and and briars. A timely mowing can encourage the seeding of some species while eliminating less desirable ones.

Mowing is a subject unto itself. I have used a scythe in the past, just to get a taste of peasant life and because I greatly admire the medieval look of the thing – that sinuous curve of handle and elegant grim-reaper blade. But scythes require great finesse in their use, which I soon

ABOVE AND OPPOSITE: *Lupines are one of the more durable flowers, a valuable trait in a meadow setting, where less tenacious plants soon vanish.*

A small meadow garden of heirloom annuals, including false Queen Anne's lace, bachelor's buttons, and painted tongue (Salpiglossis sinuata). *Barrett House, New Hampshire.*

discovered I lacked, and, with my stony ground, constant sharpening. I now prefer to mow my meadow with somewhat less antique means: my old Ford tractor and jerryrigged John Deere cutter-bar mower. *Prefer* is actually understating the case, as this is one gardening maintenance task that I truly love – so much so that all I have to do is walk by the tractor parked in the barn and catch a whiff of its *odeur naturelle,* a unique aroma of sun-ripened rusted metal mingled with leaking crankcase oil and old tires, and I feel a great rush of summer mowing nostalgia.

The sensation of mowing with this long-suffering workhorse is uncannily like being in a small boat as it plows through the masses of flowers and tall grasses rippling and swaying in the wind. Sprays of green grasshoppers and black crickets, clouds of orange skippers and blue hairstreaks, burst over the bow as the tractor rolls on through the green swells. Truth be told, I mostly keep a meadow garden just to have an excuse to partake in this annual summer ritual, to relish the chatter of the mower, the sudden gusts of cool wind on sunburned skin, the swooping and feinting of the swallows and purple martins defending their birdhouses as I carefully maneuver around them, and the singular sweet fragrance of just-mown meadow grass that spills from the flashing cutter bar in my wake. This is meadow gardening at its best.

OPPOSITE: No meadow garden is complete without a birdhouse for swallows or purple martins or, preferably, bluebirds.

FOLLOWING SPREAD: *The woodland garden at Monticello.*

MY KIND *of* GARDEN

I've often wish'd that I had clear,

For life, six hundred pounds a year;

A handsome house to lodge a friend,

A river at my garden's end,

A terrace walk, and half a rood

Of land set out to plant a wood.

~ ALEXANDER POPE

GARDENS HAVE ALWAYS BEEN the stuff of dreams and wishes. We can all picture in our mind's eye what our own personal Eden would be. My most pleasant gardening hours are often the ones that take place in my imagination, where an old iron gate overgrown with roses swings open with a welcoming creak and a worn and mossy path beckons; where water splashes with a refreshing sibilance and the delphiniums grow eight feet tall, unblemished and unbent by the harsh winds of reality.

The disparity between the garden I have labored over and the garden that dwells in my mind is so great you would think I would have long since thrown in the trowel. And while hope, like crabgrass, may spring eternal, it is not hope that leads me on. I work under no delusion that someday all that I admire in the horticultural handiwork of others – the

PAGE 152 AND OPPOSITE:
I've often wished for a garden with a venerable iron gate and a lush planting of bright perennials.

FINAL SPREAD:
Stream garden, Glencoe Farm, Pennsylvania.

mellow brick walls dripping with lavender wisteria, the bright beds of vibrant lupines and flashing poppies, the limpid pools dotted with ivory water lilies – will miraculously spring forth from my meager efforts like Jack's wondrous beanstalk from a few paltry seeds.

The true wonder is that the simple act of growing a handful of plants in a setting of my own creation can yield such deeply felt satisfaction. For I have discovered that given enough modest success, even gardening at my level of ineptitude fulfills this basic human desire. At the end of a day spent puttering around in my garden, I take a minute to savor the simple joys of the endeavor. For this moment I choose to ignore the yellow leaves wilting on the hollyhocks, the small rodent snacking on the lily buds, and the mildew flourishing on the phlox – not to mention the neglected irises begging to be deadheaded and the collection of still unplanted perennials eyeing me reproachfully from their plastic pots.

The sun has dropped behind the maples and the light is soft and golden. There is a pleasing sufficiency of bloom, and the water trickles into the trough with perfect pitch. My dirt-caked fingers have the fresh smell of loam about them, my knees haven't failed me, and my shoulders register just the right amount of fatigue; they have been well but not over used. I take a long, all-encompassing, all-forgiving look. This is my kind of garden, and it is just as rewarding as any I might imagine could be.

Acknowledgments

Without the generosity of the gardeners and owners who allowed me to photograph their horticultural efforts, this book could not have been published. I am particularly indebted to Frank and Anne Cabot, whose gardens in La Malbaie, Quebec, and Cold Spring, New York, have been especially inspiring. Also, I would like to give special thanks to Morrell and Genevieve Trimble, of Afton Villa, Louisiana, who have contributed much to both the art of southern gardening and the art of true southern hospitality, as well as to Peter and Su Hua Newton, of Newton Vineyards, St. Helena, California, who gave me free rein in their vineyard garden and the use of a 150-foot crane and operator to photograph it from a memorable vantage point.

Many of my fellow Vermonters have been more than generous with their time and gardens, foremost among them J. Watson Webb, Jr., Joe Eck and Wayne Winterrowd of North Hill fame, Louis and Nancy Hill, and, of course, Tasha Tudor, whose cottage-style garden continues to grow in beauty and repute. In Connecticut, I am grateful to George Schoellkopf, Dick and Herbert Redfield, Missy Stevens and Tommy Simpson, and Kit and Martin Sagendorf for giving me the chance to capture their masterful efforts on film. I have also been fortunate in having the opportunity to photograph Sir John Thouron's magnificent gardens at Glencoe Farm, in Pennsylvania, and Mary and the late Thomas Hall's oceanside garden on Mount Desert Island, Maine. Others who have been very helpful include Brent and Becky Heath of the Daffodil Mart, Gloucester, Virginia; Celia Jones and Jan Grigsby of the Sisters' Bulb Farm, Gibsland, Louisiana; and Holly Shimizu, Russell Morash, and the staff at the Victory Garden in Lexington, Massachusetts.

In addition to the private gardens mentioned above, numerous gardens held by foundations and open to the public have been an invaluable resource for much of my photography. I am very grateful to the trustees, directors, and staff of these institutions for all their assistance and especially for letting me photograph at the early and late hours that produce the best results. These include Chesterwood, Colonial Williamsburg, Monticello, Old Westbury Gardens, Callaway Gardens, The Mission House (The Trustees of Reservations), Barrett House (Society for the Preservation of New England Antiquities), Villa Vizcaya, Agecroft Hall, Virginia House, The William Paca Garden, Longwood Gardens, Winterthur, The Saint-Gaudens National Historic Site (National Park Service), and The National Trust in Great Britain and all the other European gardens, both public and private, that graciously allowed me access.

I am further indebted to Tom Cooper, the editor of *Horticulture*, and to Nancy Lindemeyer, editor-in-chief, and Tovah Martin, garden editor of *Victoria*, who sent me on the far-flung assignments that garnered many of these photographs. John Preston, Tom Longfellow, and the rest of the crew at Slide Specialists, Lebanon, New Hampshire, get special thanks for their flawless and timely work in the lab, processing the hundreds of rolls of film I brought back from these trips. Frances Tenenbaum, my editor at Houghton Mifflin Company, has been a welcome voice of encouragement and good judgment, shepherding this project to its completion. Terry McAweeney also deserves well-earned credit for the artful production of this book. In addition, I would like to express my appreciation for the diligent efforts on my behalf of my agent, Colleen Mohyde. Thanks go to my stepdaughter, Willa, as well, for helping me untangle the mysteries of my computer. For her it was child's play.

Finally, and above all, I am doubly grateful to my wife, Susan, first for the beautiful design of this book, but even more for her invaluable insights, constant support, and patient understanding, which made it all possible.

As is the garden such is the gardener.

A man's nature runs either to herbs or weeds.

~ FRANCIS BACON